The Country Home

T I M E - L I F E   B O O K S

Alexandria, Virginia

The
Country
Home

a room-by-room look
at country style

A REBUS BOOK

C O N T E N T S

The Bathroom

Warm and Cozy · *Feminine Style* · *Scented Floral Waters*
Attention to Detail · *French Fantasy* · *Pretty and Private*
Crafting a Fabric-Covered Screen · *Painterly Touches*
The Richness of Wood

120

The Hall

Painted Patterns · *Inviting Entryways*
Showcases for Collectibles
Country Mudrooms · *A Doorknob Coatrack*
Carriage House Charm

140

The Porch

Versatile Wicker · *A Natural Setting* · *Traditional Lanterns*
Porch Living · *Casual Refinement*
An Introduction to Wicker ·*Rustic Retreats*
An Outdoor Room

154

CREDITS

170

INDEX

172

ACKNOWLEDGMENTS

175

Welcome to country style, a personal approach to decorating that expresses warmth, tradition, and an appreciation of handcraftsmanship. Unlike many other decorating styles, the country look is not linked to one historical period or limited by a particular geographical region. But while it accommodates many varied tastes and cultural influences, it is always cozy, familiar, and inviting. More than anything else, rooms decorated in the country style make you feel at home.

Although comfort is synonymous with country decorating, the idea of actually making a home comfortable is a relatively modern concern. Typical living quarters in Europe prior to the 17th century consisted of large, single chambers, open to the rafters. Here, all the functions of daily life—cooking, eating, sleeping, entertaining, negotiating business, even housing livestock— took place. Houses were meant as shelter, and the concepts of privacy and homeyness—at least as we know them today—were unfamiliar. When the first European settlers came to America, they were so concerned with basic survival that comfort was a secondary consideration. Only after the late 17th century, when private households began to focus on family life, did the contemporary idea of the house as home develop.

Today the home is not only a symbol of family life and well-being, but also a place to express one's individual tastes. To this end, "country" is perhaps the most flexible of all decorating styles. It encompasses the rustic and the tailored, the casual and the formal, the simple and the elaborate with equal ease. It gracefully incorporates the design traditions of such varied cultures as the English, Dutch, French, Germans, Scandinavians, and American Indians, among others. And it works just as well in a modern apartment with white walls and bleached floors as it does in a restored 18th-century farmhouse.

The Country Home introduces you to the many facets of country style with a room-by-room look at the major living areas of the home. In each chapter you will see how homeowners throughout America have used country furniture and accessories to make personal statements. The rich variety of decorating ideas you will encounter here proves that there are no set rules for country style: the choices available are limited only by your imagination.

Whether you are a newcomer to the country look or a long-time admirer, you can use this book as inspiration for decorating —or simply accessorizing—your own home. You will find rooms that display an effective mix of fine antiques and contemporary pieces, and those that are furnished with period reproductions. There are rooms that are intentionally spare, designed to display one or two valuable heirlooms, and rooms that overflow with flea-market finds, decoys, and quilts. Still others—decorated with lace, bric-a-brac, and richly upholstered furniture—embrace the flowery romanticism of the Victorian era. Yet despite their differences, every room in this book shares a common bond: the warmth that is the heart of country style.

The Living Room

*warm and welcoming,
a comfortable room for gathering
and entertaining*

No room better expresses the warm, convivial spirit of country style than the living room, a place for relaxing with family, for entertaining friends, or for spending a quiet evening by the hearth. But the welcoming living room that we enjoy today is a relatively recent development. In early American homes, where each room served many purposes, there was no specific place for social gatherings. The "best room," also known variously as the parlor, drawing room, or salon, evolved in the 1800s, but not until this century did the notion of the living room as a place for relaxation and comfort fully emerge.

Friendly and inviting, today's country living room accommodates both the formal and informal. While many of the rooms on the following pages are clearly the best room of the house, not one suffers from stuffiness. And while each reflects the personal touch of the people who live there, every one is carefully arranged with an eye toward the comfort of all who enter.

The glow from candles and hearth warms a country-style living room.

To express their "love of primitives" the owners of this 1960s ranch house found rustic pieces like the Ohio jelly cupboard above for their country-style living room. The cupboard, which retains its original blue paint and wooden latches, not only provides household storage, but also offers display space for a collection of wooden pantry boxes.

The setting for this homespun living room is a suburban Ohio ranch house. But it is the authentic architectural detail and convincing mix of antiques and reproductions that transports the room back to the 1800s.

The owners installed hand-hewn beams, random-width floorboards, and planked wall paneling to set the scene for rustic furnishings like the 1820 farm table at right, used here as a dining table, and the jelly cupboard above.

Drawn close to the hearth is an upholstered settle: the high backs of such benches were originally designed to keep out drafts. A reproduction, this settle is covered with a traditional plaid and draped with an 1851 linen jacquard coverlet. The kneeling bench placed in front now functions as a footrest.

Preserving the Past

Gathered from the homeowners' garden and dried, silvery-gray artemisia hangs from the mantel at left. Adding texture and interest to the beamed ceiling are a variety of New England market baskets interspersed among more dried plants and flowers.

A Carefree Mix

The owner of this Manhattan apartment combined her furnishings and accessories with a free hand to create a relaxed country-style living room in the city. The formal Chippendale-style secretary and rustic coffee table mix easily with casual upholstered pieces. And the banister-back chair—a family heirloom —offsets the inexpensive wicker rockers that the homeowner bought at a flea market.

The eclectic furnishings are unified by soft colors: related shades of pink were chosen for the walls and moldings, and additional pastels are picked up in the floral fabrics, rug, hatboxes, and quilts. The molded mantelpiece, which depicts a stylized Renaissance coat of arms, was hand-painted to coordinate with the color scheme. The delicate tiles were custom-made.

A hand-painted polychrome fireplace, left, dominates this lighthearted city living room.

Three different chintzes— on the chair, pillow cover, and hanging quilt above— mix well because they are related by color. Chintz, made of glazed cotton, derives its name from the Indian word chitta, which referred to the hand-painted and printed fabrics made in that country during the 17th century.

THE SEASONAL FIREPLACE

While a blazing wintertime fire is sure to draw attention to your hearth, the fireplace can still remain the focus of a room even when warmer weather prevails. By decorating your entire fireplace—hearth as well as mantel—you can make it an attractive showplace year round.

The suggestions for seasonal fireplace decorations on these pages are just that, suggestions. Indeed, when combined imaginatively, any accessories or mementos you have can effectively transform your fireplace.

Welcome spring, for example, by lining up a row of whirligigs on the mantel and placing a pretty painted fireboard on the hearth. Or consider attaching a fluorescent plant light to the damper and cultivating a spring flower garden.

When summer arrives, you might display a school of fish decoys on the

To achieve the springtime look above, layer chintz napkins on the mantel to make a colorful skirt, then set framed botanical prints on top. For the summery mantel at right, use assorted bottles as vases for individual stems to make a carefree garden. Displaying a variety of flowers creates a more imaginative "landscape."

mantel, or spread out a selection of antique fans. Put a large vase or a rustic bucket between the andirons and fill it with fresh gladiolas or other tall flowers to brighten up the space. Or consider removing the andirons and replacing them with an arrangement of interesting "hearth sculptures," such as weather vanes or whimsical folk-art farm animals.

For an autumnal feeling, place stirrup-cups, brass hunting horns, or English sporting prints on the mantel or hearth. Redware plates or trays painted with warm golds, rusts, and greens can also provide fall color.

And as winter takes hold, light a fire and line the mantel with tiny framed silhouettes. A grouping of antique toys will ready the fireplace for Christmas, and chains of cranberries, dried apples, and cinnamon sticks hung from the mantel will add holiday charm.

Celebrate autumn, above, by combining majolica and creamware plates with pears on the mantel, and hanging dried herbs and flowers below. Use more dried flowers to fill a basket for the hearth. The winter look at left comes from a collection of candlesticks casually arranged on a delicate lace runner. Keep firewood close at hand in a copper boiler.

Log Cabin Style

Called the art of the common man, American folk art— both old and new—is often decorated with designs based on familiar and sentimental themes. The hand-carved horse at top displays tiny hearts, while the horse at bottom borrows its colors and pattern from the American flag. Both are contemporary pieces.

The owner of this log cabin hideaway in a Washington, D.C., suburb was initially attracted to the rustic house because it reminded her of the Idaho ranch where she had been raised. She felt, though, that the twenty-year-old structure—which had been built from a kit by a previous resident—was dark and needed a more open feeling.

Her first step was to brighten the living room by painting the ceiling white, installing sky-lights, and adding large multipaned windows on either side of the fireplace, opposite. With more natural light and expanded views of the cabin's wooded property, the large room is now sunny and welcoming.

She then created the warm decor around comfortable furnishings, including denim-covered armchairs and a colorful kilim rug she bought in Pakistan, and added an unusual combination of folk art gathered on her travels around the world. On the hearth stands a Guatemalan wood carving—a primitive rendering of a Spanish coat of arms—which serves as a decorative screen when the fireplace is not in use. Atop the mantel are Czechoslovakian ceramics and a horse weather vane made in America.

Equally at home in the roughhewn setting is the owner's collection of miniature wooden houses. Displayed on an antique pie safe, the West Virginia log cabin above is complete with front porch, horses, feed sacks, cacti, washtub, and the requisite outhouse. The handmade contemporary flag quilt behind the cabin was a gift from a friend.

In this rustic living room, favorite belongings, like the miniature log cabin above and the painted covered wagon scene on the wall by the fireplace opposite, remind the owner of her western roots. With its Log Cabin pattern, the Idaho quilt is a particularly appropriate addition.

Casual and Airy

Collected for their natural beauty, abandoned birds' nests can be filled with wooden eggs, potpourri, autumn leaves, or other objects, to become attractive, unusual accessories.

Whitewashed walls and simple accessories give this small cottage living room its casual country look. To create the illusion of more space, the owner chose a plain background and kept furnishings to a minimum. Color and interest come from accessories—chintz-covered pillows, a quilt, a collection of china—that can easily be changed against the white backdrop to suit any mood.

The easy atmosphere is enhanced by a mix of antiques and yard-sale purchases cleverly put to new uses. A late-19th-century bench is now a coffee table. By the window, an old washstand serves as a pedestal for a potted plant. A turn-of-the-century English tea cloth spread over a skirt of inexpensive striped fabric transforms an old table into an elegant display piece for the Staffordshire teacups arranged on top. The pillow covers for the chair and sofa were made from remnants of old English chintz.

Natural elements have also been woven into the decor. A rug made of sisal, a durable fiber traditionally used for rope making, provides an easy-care covering for the wide-board pine floor. And the twig chair, made from branches by a contemporary artisan, is prized for its appealing individuality. Its rustic design recalls the Adirondack-style furniture made for mountain resorts and hunting lodges in the late 19th and early 20th centuries.

Above, a chintz-covered pillow softens the angular lines of the rustic twig chair, chosen to complement the nature-inspired decor. The exposed timbers over the fireplace promote the country cottage feeling.

Opposite, lightweight canvas, used to make the curtains and the sofa slipcover, and romantic floral accents in the chintz and the botanical prints, contribute to the casual look of this country living room. The English Staffordshire teacups date from the mid-19th century.

A Traditional Keeping Room

Utilitarian and utterly plain, hogscraper candlesticks like those above were common utensils in 18th- and 19th-century homes. According to legend, the name refers to their saucerlike bases, which could be sharpened and used to scrape the bristles off butchered hogs. Such candlesticks were generally made of tinned sheet iron and were often banded with brass.

U sed for both cooking and heating, the fireplace was the most important feature of the early American keeping room, an all-purpose space that accommodated a broad range of activities, from dining to sleeping.

In this spacious midwestern version of a keeping room (which contains the cozy sitting area at left and the small library above), the fireplace was designed to dominate. An exact replica of the walk-in hearth in an 18th-century Connecticut tavern, it measures five feet tall and ten feet wide. Here, the position of the hearth clearly determines the furniture arrangement: the sofa and wing chair are pulled in close for warmth.

Continued

At one end of the keeping room, a library area, above, houses 18th- and 19th-century leather-bound books. Defining the space are an early-19th-century tavern table and pair of Windsor chairs set on a hooked rug made in the late 1800s.

In the large keeping room at left, the hand-braided rug unifies a cozy hearthside furniture arrangement.

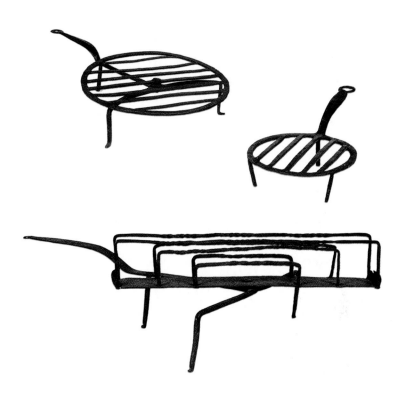

In spring and summer, when the homeowners aren't experimenting with hearth cooking and baking, the brick-lined fireplace becomes a handsome showcase for a collection of early American hearth utensils.

Hung on the heavy wooden lintel that spans the top of the hearth are a tube-shaped tin candle box and wrought-iron-handled brass ladles and a spatula. Mounted inside are long iron trammels designed to support cooking pots and kettles, which can be hung at different levels using the adjustable saw-toothed iron ratchets.

A trio of stoneware storage jugs makes a pretty flower display on one side of the expansive hearth, and a Norwegian spinning wheel and a three-legged milking stool decorate the other.

The rustic chandelier that hangs overhead was made by a previous owner of the house from an old staircase spindle. Its gracefully curved tin arms hold hand-dipped candles.

Built with century-old paving bricks from a Minneapolis street, the huge fireplace at left displays early cooking implements.

Although 18th-century wrought-iron cooking utensils look unwieldy, they were actually designed to make kitchen tasks easier. Each of the utensils above served a specific purpose: the round broilers, one rotary (top left), the other stationary (top right), were used to grill meats, fish, or poultry. The swivel-base toaster (bottom) turned to brown slices of bread.

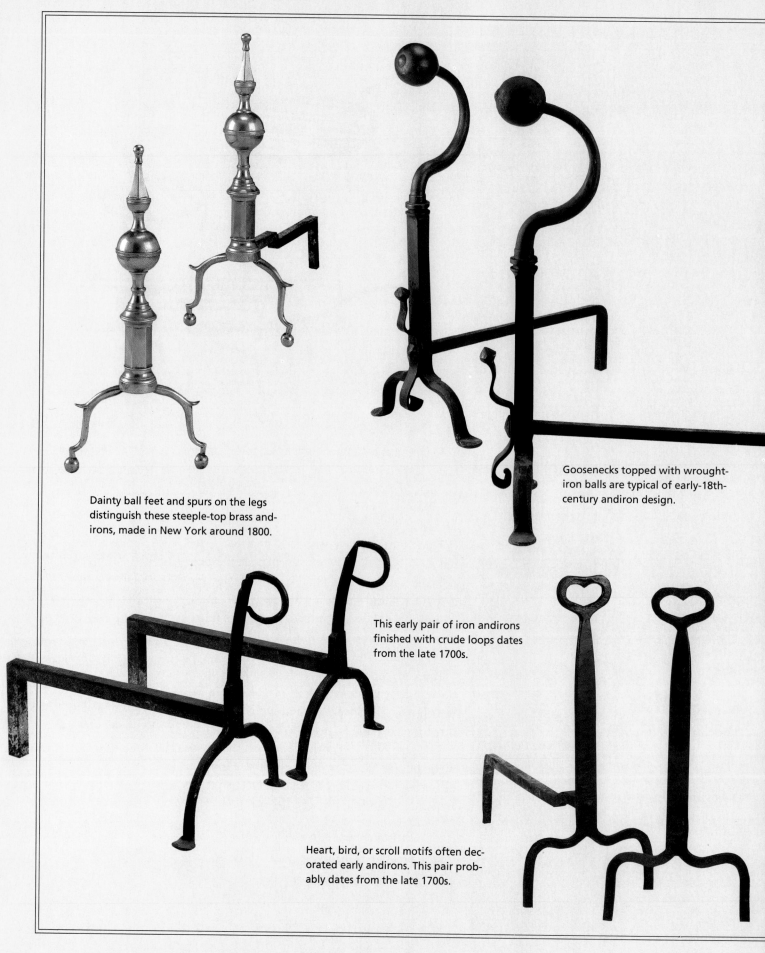

Dainty ball feet and spurs on the legs distinguish these steeple-top brass andirons, made in New York around 1800.

Goosenecks topped with wrought-iron balls are typical of early-18th-century andiron design.

This early pair of iron andirons finished with crude loops dates from the late 1700s.

Heart, bird, or scroll motifs often decorated early andirons. This pair probably dates from the late 1700s.

ANDIRONS IN AMERICA

Brass urn finials lend elegance to these c. 1790 knife-blade andirons with flat iron shafts.

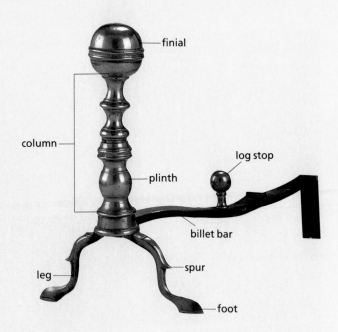

finial

column

plinth

log stop

billet bar

spur

leg

foot

These brass andirons, made in New York around 1800, are decorated with double-lemon finials and ball feet.

Andirons are among the house-hold implements that serve us today as well as they did our ances-tors. Designed to hold logs off the floor of the fireplace for more effi-cient burning, the L-shaped tools—known variously as andirons, hand-irons, cob-irons, and firedogs—were commonly used in Europe as early as the 15th century.

Little is known about the pro-duction of andirons in the American colonies during the 1600s. At least one cast-iron example, topped with a cherub's head, was discovered at the Jamestown settlement. But like other early andirons found in America, it is generally believed to have been made in England.

Whatever their origins, the first andirons used in this country were made of cast or wrought iron with simple uprights, which might be looped to hold a roasting spit.

During the 1700s, the role and design of the fireplace—and its ac-cessories—began to change. While kitchen hearths were still used for cooking, parlor fireplaces became smaller, more formalized and dec-orative, calling for more elegant andirons. During this time, andirons made of wrought iron ornamented with brass finials came into wide use.

Like other household accessories, 18th-century andirons reflected the trends in furniture designs of the day. Some, for example, displayed curved cabriole legs, as elegant as any that might be seen on a Queen Anne or Chippendale chair. Others reflected such period details as ball-and-claw feet, and finials shaped like urns or fruit, set on columns.

The andirons shown here are just a few examples of the many designs that appeared during Amer-ica's early years.

The Charm of Flowers

Combining large-scale floral patterns, which takes a strong color sense and a keen eye, was how the owner of this country-style living room chose to decorate the converted century-old Long Island barn that she uses as a summer house. In this light, airy living room, remodeled from two smaller rooms and opened up with raised ceilings and new French doors, the patterns and accessories were selected with particular care.

Because color shades can change significantly under different lighting conditions, the homeowner, who is an interior decorator, began by bringing fabric, paint, and wallpaper samples into the house and checking how they looked during the day and at night.

Although her final choices include a variety of colors and patterns, the decor is tied together by one dominant motif—the blooming rose. This flower is repeated in related tones of pink in the draperies, rug, chair, and ruffled pillow in the sitting area above, as well as in the fabrics, needlepoint rug, and even on the lampshades, at right.

Details also play a role in the room's decor: the trompe l'oeil "tassled" wallpaper borders on the valances over the bamboo blinds, for example, playfully echo the fringe on the drapery valances as well as on the sofas. *Continued*

In this pretty room, accessories like the English platters on the wall above and the Sèvres tureen on the lacquered table at right accent the rose theme.

Majolica, *an anglicized name for the Italian tin-glazed earthenware known as "maiolica," also refers to a type of earthenware colored with lead glazes. American-made majolica— kiln-fired in factories and decorated almost exclusively by young women—was particularly popular in this country during the 19th century. The basket-weave pitcher, top, dates from the mid-1800s; the new pitcher, bottom, resembles a tree branch and is decorated with oak leaves and acorns.*

Installed by the homeowner, the paneled mantel above was designed to look like an original part of this hundred-year-old house.

Located at one end of the same room, the fireplace above also echoes the floral motif. Imported from England, the ceramic tiles, hand-painted with roses, make an elegant facing for the surround. When the fireplace is not in use, a Victorian bamboo fire screen with embroidered flowers stands in front.

Although the overall feeling of the room is soft and delicate, the pieces of sporting art also displayed here fit in comfortably. The painting over the mantel, by the 19th-century English artist Benjamin Herring, Sr., is complemented by the equestrian prints hung in the corner. Polished pewter tankards ornament the mantel.

Simply Elegant

The owners of this recently built colonial-style farmhouse delight in its simple elegance and authentic architectural details. And, in keeping with the austere beauty of the house, they decorated the living room with a careful mix of 18th-century-style furniture.

The camelback sofa, left, and the wing chairs, upholstered with a traditional flame-stitch-pattern fabric, show classic Chippendale designs. Although reproductions, they go well with the owners' antiques, including the early-18th-century Queen Anne tavern table in front of the sofa and the sturdy banister-back armchair.

The canvas floor cloth is also an appropriate addition, as such painted "rugs" were commonly used in colonial homes. Often they were decorated to resemble floor materials: a checkered pattern like this one was used to imitate tiles.

Blending into the decor are two American portraits. The one over the mantel was painted around 1830 by a Maine artist; the young girl, above, is a copy of a well-known work by Ammi Phillips, one of the most prolific country portrait painters of the 19th century.

The fine detailing in this reproduction 18th-century farmhouse living room shows in the encased beams and paneled doors, left. The portrait above was copied by one of the homeowners from a 19th-century original.

COUNTRY FABRICS

TRADITIONAL

woven cotton   woven cotto

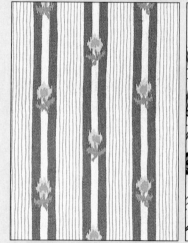

CASUAL

printed cotton   printed cot

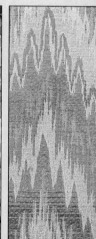

ROMANTIC

cotton chintz   woven co

W hen you are thinking of up-holstering or slipcovering your country furniture—perhaps a wing chair like the one here, or some other piece—it is important to consider the mood you want to create. Often the fabric you choose can determine the tenor of a room.

In colonial times, the upholstery used on wing chairs, settees, sofas, day beds, and many types of side chairs was made from a surprising variety of materials, including silk, leather, embroidered canvas, printed cottons, and homespuns. Today these materials—and dozens of others—continue to be popular choices for country furniture.

When selecting any upholstery fabric, you should consider color, pattern, weave, and texture. Tapestry weaves, worked with rich, often varicolored, patterns, for example, have a characteristically traditional feeling, as do many cottons decorated with classic bird, animal, and floral motifs. Dark colors can have a formal effect, while small, closely repeated designs, ginghams, and nubby homespuns will lend your furniture a more casual feeling. And for a romantic touch, there are pretty chintzes splashed with bright flowers.

The swatches at right offer ideas for fabrics that can give your furniture a country look.

The patterns shown are one third actual size. See page 170 for additional information.

woven blend

printed cotton

printed cotton

woven blend

printed cotton

woven cotton

woven blend

printed cotton

cotton chintz

cotton chintz

printed blend

cotton chintz

Cool Summer Colors

A casual mix of patterns, incorporating stripes, checks, and florals, was used to achieve the lighthearted decor in the living room at right. For a fresh, unified look, the homeowner painted all the walls white and added white accessories, including the candles and lampshades.

A pleasing palette of white, pink, and green gives this country-style beach house a fresh summer look all year round. Light, bright, and filled with flowers, the living room takes a cheerful decorative cue from the floral-patterned upholstery that covers the cushioned sofa and matching throw pillows. The pink-striped pillows and the green-checked woven rug were chosen for contrast.

The summertime theme is repeated in the fresh flowers clustered into informal bouquets and placed throughout the room. And dried

Antique botanical prints, such as the 1810 English engraving at top, are delicate, beautiful, and often expensive. Creative homeowners can make their own "botanicals" by framing pressed-flower arrangements like the one at bottom, composed of coral-bells, columbine, and star-of-Bethlehem.

flowers, too, work as part of the design: the "botanicals" on the walls are made from pressed flowers mounted in plain wooden frames. Hung in long rows, they make a simple yet striking arrangement.

To enhance the casual look, the homeowner mixed rustic outdoor furnishings—all painted a unifying dark green—with her upholstered pieces. Simple lace-trimmed cafe curtains keep the feeling light, and the French doors by the dining area let in welcome breezes throughout the summer months.

Charmed by its intimate scale, the owners of this converted century-old one-room schoolhouse furnished it as a weekend retreat, combining rich colors and comfortable furniture in the snug living room.

Pulled close to the hearth, right, "host" and "hostess" club chairs and an 18th-century cricket table of bleached oak define a cozy sitting area where the homeowners can read and dine. To enhance the warm feeling of the room, they chose a color scheme dominated by deep red, which appears in the checked and flowered chair upholstery and in the flat-woven kilim rug. The floors were painted a complementary green, and then spattered with red and yellow to provide added texture and heightened color dimension.

The accessories, each a beautiful object in itself, were selected to add interest without overwhelming the small, quiet room. A collection of majolica, including the butterfly plates mounted on the chimney breast, displays the dark, earth-tone glazes often used on this pottery. The stenciled picture, which has been framed in bird's-eye maple, contributes its own naive charm to the setting.

Purposely subdued to maintain a warm feeling, the illumination in this room comes mostly from candlelight and firelight. The electric lighting is limited to small table lamps that are topped with dark shades to yield a soft glow.

This intimate living room is part of a converted one-room schoolhouse. Unusual accessories like the 18th-century wooden bowl decorated with iron studs, above, give the room its unique character. The carved deer came from Burma.

Crafting Fine Design

The owners of this New England dining room share a strong interest in American craftsmanship that extends to furniture and textiles and to everyday housewares. Attracted by quality and design, they collect and use antiques and fine reproduction pieces and enjoy displaying both in the same room.

The stenciled linen tablecloth, as well as the pewter plates, tab-handled basins, spoons, and footed salts that they use to set their dining table, for example, are the works of two different con-

temporary Pennsylvania craftspeople. Recalling an especially popular type of colonial stemware, the hand-blown trumpet-shaped glasses are also reproductions.

Many of the other furnishings in the room, however, are antiques, including the painted banister-back chairs and the blanket chest—all New England pieces from the mid-1700s. The unusual artwork above the chest is a crewel-embroidered chair-seat cover from the Queen Anne period, framed for display.

Before fine pottery and porcelain became widely available in the late 1700s, pewter pieces like the footed bowl, top, and dome-lidded pitcher, bottom, were commonly used as tableware.

A "twisted rope" wallpaper border, opposite, accents the trim in this dining room, where furnishings include antiques as well as new pieces such as the smoke-grained candlesticks opposite and above.

OLD
COUNTRY
DINNERWARE

Whether reserved for display or put to use, vintage dinnerware continues to have a place in the country dining room today. Some examples that are still available include Canton, first shipped to the West from China in the 1600s, and creamware, an inexpensive earthenware imported in large quantities from England after the Revolution.

In the 19th century, equally desirable additions to the table were blue and white willowware, produced in the Staffordshire region of England, and the brightly patterned pottery known as Gaudy Dutch, also produced in Staffordshire.

Among the many types of country dinnerware made in America during the 19th and early 20th centuries were spongeware and spatterware ceramics, and graniteware, generally made of lightweight enameled iron or steel.

Top row, left to right: Staffordshire creamware, c. 1800; creamware, spinach and egg pattern, c. 1760; Staffordshire, c. 1840; Historical Staffordshire, c. 1830; Historical Staffordshire, c. 1825. **Middle row:** willowware, c. 1929-1942; Gaudy Dutch, carnation pattern, c. 1810; graniteware, c. 1900; Mason's ironstone, c. 1815; Flow Blue, Amish snowflake pattern, c. 1850. **Bottom row:** Canton, c. 1830-1840; majolica, basket weave and leaves pattern, c. 1870; Staffordshire, cut-sponge camellia pattern, c. 1850; spongeware, c. 1880; Staffordshire spatterware, tulip pattern, c. 1830.

NEW COUNTRY DINNERWARE

I f antique dinnerware doesn't suit your style, or your pocketbook, you can still get the country look with new pottery or china. Many of the types you can purchase today take their inspiration from antique textile and porcelain patterns.

Among the choices are handcrafted reproductions of 18th- and 19th-century pottery, such as redware, which are being made and decorated using materials and techniques similar to those employed by early potters. Other manufacturers are using modern technology to copy or update old patterns.

The new dinnerware at left will give you just a few ideas for setting your country table. Consider mixing styles, colors, and patterns rather than choosing just one.

Top row, left to right: plate from Fruit Collection by Mottahedeh; "Colore" by Vietri; "Jade," Normandie Series, by Loneoak & Co.; "No 24," Genre Ancien Series, by Quimper Faience; "Red Leaf" by Barbara Eigen. **Middle row:** slip-trailed redware by Jeff White; "Rose Basket" by Gear; "Farm House Charger" by Jeff White; "Vieux Luxembourg" by Villeroy & Boch; "Blue Agate" by Bennington Potters. **Bottom row:** "The Vineyard" by Marion Grebow; "Blue Sky," Mesa Series, by Dansk; "Hunter" by Victoria and Richard MacKenzie-Childs, Ltd.; "Victoria's Garden" by Arita for Gear; plate from Victorian Garden Collection by Trifles. See page 170 for additional information.

Tall, fancy banister-back chairs like the one above reflect the new elegance and sophistication that characterized 18th-century design. This painted armchair, made in Maine around 1750, is particularly notable for its finely carved crest. With its splint-woven seat and lathe-turned members, it is typical of the William and Mary style.

Although located in a new house, this traditional dining room has the hospitable feeling of a country inn. The room draws much of its appeal from the fireplace, set off by richly grained cherry paneling, and from the handsome furnishings clustered near the hearth.

The centerpiece here, though, is the 18th-century hutch-table (the top flips back to make a high-back chair), which retains the original red paint on its base. The 18th-century chairs include a comb-back Windsor armchair and two banister-back chairs with scalloped crest rails. The Windsor is draped with a fire bag, a canvas sack traditionally kept on hand for speedy packing of valuables in the event of a house fire. The hooked rug displays a Broken Glass pattern.

True to Tradition

The subdued lighting in the dining room at left comes mainly from the rare early-19th-century tin chandelier (its large size suggests that it originally hung in a church or meetinghouse) and two sconces, one mirrored and the other backed with reflective tin.

City Casual

Bands of dark tiles provide strong accents on the cream-colored tile walls in this casual Manhattan dining room. The wares displayed on the table include green ironstone and yellowware pottery pieces and a pair of animal-shaped cookie jars from the 1940s.

The owners of this lighthearted dining room wanted an informal eating area that would be compatible with their late-19th-century New York City apartment. To create an old-fashioned "back of the house" feeling, they used simple, cream-colored tiles and wood wainscoting on the walls, and added a paneled partition to make a cozy alcove for their dining table and chairs. Chosen for their whimsical appeal, the painted wooden cutouts of animals and birds mounted on the wainscoting were originally attached to an antique crib.

The open-top cupboard above was custom-made to display kitchen and table wares, as well as a collection of nursery toys that are particularly well suited to the room's playful atmosphere. Among the owners' favorite collectibles are their eight colorful automobile teapots from England, a bowl of papier-mâché Easter eggs, and the carved wooden rabbits that rest atop the case. The large, colorful prints are seed company advertisements from the 1940s.

Among the unusual collectibles in the custom-made cupboard above are a group of colorful 1920s teapots shaped like cars. Their license plates read "T 4 2."

An Artful Blend

A straightforward decor distinguishes this engaging dining room, in which the homeowners have successfully combined new and old furnishings with a collection of handcrafted folk-art pieces.

The work of a contemporary designer, the walnut trestle table and the matching fan-back Windsor chairs are conscious adaptations of familiar early American furniture types. Their simple forms and hand-rubbed finishes are a natural complement to the antiques in the room, including the painted apothecary chest above. Made in New York State around 1840, this striking chest, used now for both storage and display, contains fifty drawers that are graduated in size from row to row.

Equally interesting in design are a painted Gothic Revival bench and a 19th-century copper weather vane, which has been mounted on a tall stand to simulate its customary rooftop perch. By the window, a Pennsylvania tavern table holds a primitive tiger carving crafted from a poplar log. The piece beside it is a whirligig made by a Pennsylvania artisan in 1890.

Among the country furnishings in this contemporary suburban dining room is the antique chest above, originally used by an apothecary to hold such medicinal supplies as powders and tablets. The walnut dining table and chairs at right, and the light fixture above the table, are new.

Country Formal

The owners of the Connecticut dining room at right selected floral fabrics for the draperies and wing chairs and painted the walls a unifying red to give the traditional room a bright feeling. The pewter chandelier is a contemporary reproduction of an 18th-century piece.

Floral fabrics and bright colors bring a relaxed country feeling to this handsome traditional dining room. Although the owners have selected formal furnishings, such as the Chippendale side chairs and Queen Anne tall chest, the room is still friendly and inviting.

An unexpected addition are the wing chairs, used instead of more conventional armchairs at the head and foot of the table. While such upholstered pieces were uncommon in 18th- and 19th-century dining rooms because they were too expensive to risk staining with food,

Blue and white porcelain, produced by decorating a white clay body with cobalt underglaze, was first devised in China during the 13th century. Adopted by European potteries beginning in the 1700s, it was imported to the American colonies by the British and Dutch East India companies. The cups, top, are from England, and the gravy boat is French.

they add a look of comfort in this 20th-century setting. Ruffled valances over the draperies are a casual touch.

To tie together the different but complementary fabrics used on the draperies and the chair upholstery, the owners selected a vivid red paint for the walls. Depending on the light, the color varies from tomato red to deep crimson.

When guests are expected, the homeowners enhance the traditional mood by setting the table with damask and lace cloths and fine English and French china.

CARE OF VINTAGE LINENS

Vintage linens are lovely accessories for the dining table, but caring for them requires a touch as delicate as the fabrics themselves.

Old or fragile linens should never be washed or dried by machine or exposed to chlorine bleach. To freshen yellowed fabrics and clean lightly soiled pieces, you should hand-wash them in warm water (no hotter than 110 degrees Fahrenheit) with a mild detergent. Use a large nonaluminum bowl or basin, and fold the linens before submerging them to prevent creasing.

Stained linens need particular attention. When linens become soiled with food or wine, put cold water or club soda on the stain as a temporary measure. All stained pieces should be soaked before washing in cool water mixed with a commercial enzyme presoak product: follow the manufacturer's directions. (Presoaking is most effective for milk and other protein stains.) Do not add detergent, as it might set the stain; leave the linens undisturbed overnight.

If your linens are not especially old or fragile, you can also remove stains and whiten yellowed fabrics by boiling them. Mix a mild detergent with cold water in a large nonaluminum pot and add the linens. Bring the water to a boil, and simmer the fabrics gently for five to fifteen minutes, depending on how bad the stains are.

All linens should be rinsed carefully. Never lift pieces directly from the water, as their weight could cause them to tear. To drain after washing, let the linens fall gently into a colander. Rinse them well under cold water, and drain again.

Dry linens by blotting them gently with a clean towel, then lay them flat on dry towels; do not hang them while they are wet. Press the fabrics on a padded ironing board with a steam iron while they are still damp.

Authentic Furnishings

Homespun napkins and tab curtains, and a braided wool rug, provide color and texture in the rustic dining room at right. The collection of fine antiques includes the set of bow-back Windsor chairs around the table.

In this midwestern keeping room, feather-edged pine paneling creates a simple, rustic setting for a valued collection of 18th- and 19th-century country furniture.

Here, the owners have selected the pieces with particular care, and each is prized for its authentic detail. Both the open-top cupboard above and the corner cupboard at left bear their original paint, as does the settle-table, made around 1840. The blanket chest under the portrait also has its own intriguing detail: the date 1721 is marked with the original red paint on the bottom of the second drawer.

The 18th-century painted cupboard above, also called a dish dresser, was originally used to "dress" food before it was served at the table. Today, it is a showcase for antique and reproduction pewter pieces.

S oft colors and eclectic furnishings bring a light-spirited mood to this country breakfast room. To create an informal, cottage-style decor, the owner papered the walls with a cheery flower pattern, spatter-painted the floorboards, and added simple white swag curtains trimmed with a delicate ruffle.

A casual mix of furniture promotes the carefree feeling. The heavy oak pedestal-base table—a type popular at the turn of the 20th century for its strong design and practicality—is balanced by the more delicate painted chairs surrounding it. With urn-shaped splats and stenciled crest rails, these chairs are typical of the fancy decorated pieces that first became widely available during the early 19th century. The pine dish dryer above provides open storage for dinnerware, yellowware bowls, and baskets.

It is the striking accessories, however, that give the room its particular appeal. Perhaps the most unusual is the wrought-iron chandelier, decorated with a palm tree and camels and lit by candles. Equally charming is the majolica tableware displayed next to the window. Made in England, the 19th-century set was designed to resemble ribbon-trimmed straw hats.

This cottage-style breakfast room draws its charm from such informal furnishings as the pine dish dryer above and the Pennsylvania painted chairs at right. Whimsical touches include the collection of majolica plates and the wrought-iron chandelier.

Gracious Country

Cool colors and stainless-steel surfaces mix well with wood beams and cabinetry in the country kitchen at right. The riven, or rough, finish on the durable bluestone floor provides a practical, nonslip surface.

This handsome country kitchen incorporates sophisticated features yet remains in keeping with the century-old Long Island home to which it was added.

To achieve the gracious feeling they wanted, the owners installed false wooden ceiling beams and chose cabinetry with glass-paned doors typical of those popular at the turn of the 20th century. They also added attractive yet serviceable work areas, including easy-care stainless-steel counters and sinks. The floor, of bluestone broken into random shapes for visual interest, enhances the look of casual elegance and provides a durable surface underfoot.

At one end of the kitchen, the owners created the rather formal sitting area, above, with a symmetrical arrangement of French provincial rush-seated chairs, found in a Parisian flea market, and a Louis XV table. Mounted on the wall, the English Wedgwood dinnerware, including soup plates and large meat platters, takes the place of more traditional artwork.

Above, French country chairs and a Louis XV table, which still retains its original paint,

furnish an attractive kitchen sitting area.

Farmhouse Style

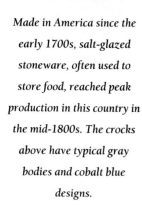

Made in America since the early 1700s, salt-glazed stoneware, often used to store food, reached peak production in this country in the mid-1800s. The crocks above have typical gray bodies and cobalt blue designs.

The kitchen in this reproduction 18th-century farmhouse is so inviting that the owner uses it as a living room. "Even though we also have a big keeping room, this is the place where everyone really wants to gather," she explains.

The warm atmosphere was achieved in part with simple, natural materials: pine paneling was chosen for the walls, ceiling, and matching cabinets, and old bricks—protected with a coat of beeswax—were used for the flooring. To blend in unobtrusively with the rustic decor, new appliances, such as the wall oven and dish-washer, were purchased in dark colors or in stainless steel with a matte finish.

Antique and handcrafted accessories were also selected to contribute to the traditional American country look. The two spice boxes flanking the cupboard above, for example, are late-19th-century pieces from the Midwest; the hand-wrought rat-tail hinges on the cabinet doors, opposite, are copies of 18th-century originals; and the braided rug, added as a warm touch, was handmade in the 1930s. The rug helps anchor the butterfly table and rod-back Windsor side chairs in the center of the room.

Antique furnishings, such as the 18th-century Pennsylvania cupboard above, designed to hold pewter tableware, are well suited to the traditional country look of this farmhouse kitchen. The table opposite is a 19th-century reproduction of an 18th-century original.

A BASKET PRIMER

If any one object could be singled out as the symbol of country style, it might be the basket. With their straightforward designs and natural materials, baskets recall a simpler life, and offer pleasing evidence of the hand at work. Their rustic textures and patterns are a natural complement to country homes, and the wide availability of baskets makes cultivating a collection an easy endeavor.

Indispensable to the routine of daily life in America's first decades, baskets were used on the farm and in the field for everything from gathering, sorting, and drying foodstuffs to storing produce and household supplies.

The baskets owned by the earliest settlers were brought from Europe or obtained through trade with American Indians. When the colonists began crafting their own baskets—generally from grasses, twigs, wood splints, and roots— they copied European and Indian techniques and designs.

During the 17th and 18th centuries, most baskets were made at home. By the early 19th century, however, the craft developed into a thriving cottage industry as enterprising basket makers began to sell their wares from door to door, in shops, or by mail order. The best-known commercial basket makers of this period were the Shakers, who by 1837 were producing over seventy types of baskets for sale outside of their own communities.

Today, Shaker baskets are just one of the many types that collectors covet. But no matter what type of basket you own, all—whether old or new—deserve thoughtful handling. Never, for example, overload a basket with anything heavy or bulky or risk damaging one by using it to hold a potted plant that might leak water.

Don't place a basket on a shelf or surface that is too narrow to accommodate it: any part that is unsupported could eventually sag and become misshapen. And always lift an old basket by holding it underneath or on the sides with both hands. The rim or handle may not be strong enough to support it.

Proper temperature and humidity are also important considerations in the care, storage, and display of baskets. Excessive heat from radiators, stoves, and fireplaces can weaken and dry out basket fibers. According to some experts, the ideal climate for baskets is a temperature between 60 and 75 degrees Fahrenheit, with a relative humidity of 40 to 60 percent. If you can't keep your house within these ranges, you should still try to prevent the conditions inside from fluctuating too much. Great variations can cause fibers to expand and contract, eventually warping the baskets.

Rustic Comfort

Comfortable and efficient, this suburban ranch house kitchen includes the compact cooking area at left and the cozy dining area decorated with primitive 19th-century furniture and handcrafted accessories on the following page.

In the practical corner work space, hardwood countertops provide a handsome, durable surface, and simple cabinets offer plenty of room for storage. Early kitchen utensils, like the mortar and pestle, slaw board, and chopper above, and the cutting boards hung by the door and placed behind the stove opposite, are not only displayed but often used. The cutting boards, for example, often double as serving trays for fresh-baked breads made by one of the owners. "We use only old stoneware and white ironstone dishes on our table," she says, "and the informal wooden cutting boards blend in perfectly."

Continued

The counter-top still life, above, is composed of early kitchen utensils, which the homeowner still uses. The slaw board, at center, works well for grating cabbage, while the hinged chopper, originally meant for tobacco, now is used for herbs. The 19th-century mortar and pestle retains its original blue paint.

Painted a soft green, classic wood cabinets bring a traditional look to the kitchen work space, left.

A Pennsylvania country cupboard, circa 1850, dominates the informal kitchen dining area above.

In the dining area above, a casual mix of furniture gives the space homey appeal. The owners prize their country furniture for its timeworn look, and they have intentionally left the original finish on pieces such as the blue-painted cupboard to enhance their value.

When entertaining guests in this cozy room, the owners often use the large sawbuck farm table and the small table by the fireplace—both late-19th-century pieces—for fireside dinners. The result is a hospitable area that, they say, "feels more like a little inn than a kitchen."

PLANTING A KITCHEN HERB GARDEN

Placed in a sunny window or under a plant light, culinary herbs can be a practical addition to any kitchen. Because their growing requirements vary, you will need to consider certain factors when choosing and tending your plants.

All herbs need light. If you don't have a window that gets about five hours of sun a day, plan to use at least one plant light as a supplement. Sage, thyme, and dill are among the herbs that need the most direct sunlight; parsley and mint do well with less.

Choose a container that has a drainage hole and is big enough to accommodate the plant's roots without crowding them. Generally, it is best to allow the soil to dry out between waterings; but some herbs, like chives, demand moist soil, and others, like lemon balm, need very dry soil.

Use a packaged potting mix for planting herbs. If you are planting chives, which grow best in extra-rich soil, add peat moss to the mix. Bay requires fast drainage, so use equal parts of sand and packaged formula. Most herbs thrive in soil supplemented by a standard houseplant fertilizer, but you should add it at half the strength and half as often as the package directions recommend. Basil is a notable exception—it should never be fertilized.

To plant any herb, spread a layer of small pebbles on the bottom of the pot and add the soil mixture until the container is half full. Center a plant in the pot and pack the soil firmly around it, filling the pot to within an inch of the top. Place the container on a saucer, and water thoroughly. You will be well on your way to a year-round supply of some of your favorite seasonings.

Warm Woods

Acomfortable gathering place for family and friends, this spacious eat-in kitchen in Connecticut draws its warmth from the rich variety of woods used throughout.

The owners picked cherry, a decorative wood prized for its fine graining, for the cabinets, and durable maple—cut on the cross grain—for the butcher-block surface on the center work island. The random-width floorboards of white pine were stained a dark color to enhance the traditional country look of the room.

The kitchen also accommodates the sunny dining nook above. The antique wood furnishings found here include a small 19th-century sawbuck table by the bay window, and a flip-top hutch table (built with the customary storage chest below), which can also serve as a seat. The burl bowl filled with rag balls and the plate resting on the table are typical of the woodenware commonly used for serving and eating during the 17th and 18th centuries. The chandelier was made by a contemporary tinsmith.

Distinguished by a combination of warm woods, this country kitchen accommodates the butcher-block

work island at left, as well as the cozy dining area above.

The Bedroom

a quiet place for relaxation
and the enjoyment of
private moments

The most personal room in the home, the country bedroom has come a long way from the makeshift arrangements of colonial days. Then sleeping quarters were generally nothing more than beds pushed to one side of the all-purpose "hall" or the parlor, which commonly doubled as the master bedroom. Only in the 19th century did the bedroom become a comfortable haven away from a home's more public rooms.

It is the concept of sanctuary that sets the tone for the bedroom today, for it is here that people are free to indulge their personal style. As you will discover in this chapter, the decor of a country bedroom need not be limited to traditional bedroom furnishings. Cherished belongings—Amish clothing simply displayed against a wall or a collection of old sewing paraphernalia set on a bedside table—can also make their own original design statements. By adding such individual touches, you can create a special room that suits your needs and tastes alone.

A Star of Bethlehem quilt is the centerpiece of a log cabin bedroom.

Playthings like those above were often meant to be educational as well as fun. The simple wooden train cars—made around 1940— can be dismantled and reassembled to acquaint children with basic geometric shapes. The 1886 board game above right helped polish spelling skills.

The casual, playful side of country style makes it especially appropriate for a child's bedroom, where bold colors and simple furnishings provide a no-fuss backdrop for plenty of pursuits other than sleeping.

Clean, dark colors help distract the eye from childhood clutter. In the cozy bedroom at right, the scheme is blue, established by the mini-print wallpaper and repeated in the jacquard coverlet and stuffed bears. To keep the dark colors from overpowering the room, the homeowners added white muslin curtains, a rag rug, and a Monkey Wrench patchwork quilt as light accents.

The durable pine furniture was also intentionally selected for its light color. The low-post bed, made by the owners, and the antique Danish armoire offer the added advantage of easy care: the natural patina of the unfinished pine only grows richer with use and scrubbing.

Antique games, and toys such as the 1930s rocking horse, add charm—and they are sturdy enough for a child's room. Wooden and stuffed toys can stand up well to years of wear, becoming even more appealing with age.

In the child's room at right, plain pine furniture and a rag rug were chosen for their durability and bright colors.

A Child's Room

Bears became the nation's most popular stuffed toys after a pair of American toymakers capitalized on Teddy Roosevelt's well-publicized refusal to shoot a cub in 1902. Due to high prices, today's bear hunters often make their own and dress them in country clothes, as above.

Victorian Romance

Corner cupboards like the 1870 midwestern piece at right were designed as space savers for cramped quarters. Built-in or movable, they still provide convenient storage, or can serve as display cases for personal treasures.

By the end of the Victorian era, a new emphasis on cleanliness and fresh air called for more "wholesome" bedrooms with soft fabrics and relatively simple furniture designed for easy maintenance. Evident in this pretty yet down-to-earth bedroom are light touches that would seldom have been seen before the late 1800s.

Instead of being draped in heavy curtains, once necessary to ward off nighttime chill, the four-poster bed is topped by a graceful serpentine tester covered in eyelet lace. The theme is elegantly echoed by a lace pillow sham, which belonged to a Victorian bride, a white coverlet, and an eyelet dust ruffle.

To maintain a consistent period decor, the owner surrounded her bed with antiques from the late 1800s, such as the velvet-upholstered armchair, the kerosene lamp (now electrified), the painted cradle, and the pull-toy horse.

And, to display things she particularly cares for, she purchased the 1870 pine corner cupboard opposite. Always left open as a showcase, it displays a bisque baby doll, a nosegay of dried flowers, and well-worn leather volumes, part of a larger collection of books. Hung on a tiny wooden hanger, the lace-trimmed dress was made for a doll in the 1870s. Nearby, a child's cradle from the 1880s has been outfitted with striped ticking as a bed for a straw-stuffed bear.

Patterned with roses, the hooked rug in front of the cupboard would have appealed to the Victorian taste for floral motifs. Rugs like these became popular in America around 1840 and were made throughout the Victorian period in a limitless range of patterns, shapes, and sizes.

A pair of hand-knit mittens hung over a cupboard as a "vase" for a spray of dried flowers adds a romantic detail to the Victorian bedroom above. The pretty canopy bed was made as a wedding gift for the homeowner by her husband.

MAKING HERBAL SACHETS

A charming way to preserve the fragrance of a country garden year-round is with a potpourri of dried herbs and flowers. Traditionally sprinkled into a decorative bowl or gathered in a handkerchief, a potpourri also makes an ideal filling for a sachet.

A sachet tucked into a chest or attached to a doorknob or hanger will perfume your bedroom and—depending on the potpourri it contains—might also double as a moth repellent. The moth potpourri recipe below includes cedar chips and lavender buds, two natural moth repellents. You'll find its fresh scent a pleasant option to mothballs. For best results, use at least two sachets per drawer and four per closet.

HERBAL MOTH POTPOURRI

Purchase these ingredients through an herbalist or at a home fragrance shop.

½ cup each, dried:
• Rosemary leaves • Lavender buds • Orrisroot •
• Cedar chips • Lemon grass • Oak moss •

Combine all ingredients in bowl. Mix gently with spoon. Yields 3 cups, or enough for six sachets.

MAKING A SACHET BAG

Easy-to-make sachet bags can be stitched from scraps of material in your sewing basket or from colorful remnants available at fabric stores. Select a natural fiber, such as cotton, linen, or wool, which will let the bag breathe. An occasional squeeze increases the scent.

• 1 piece fabric, 8 inches square (for 3½- x 5½-inch bag) •
• 1 yard ribbon, ¼ inch wide or narrower (for drawstring) •
• 7½ inches lace or ribbon (for trim) •

1. Fold fabric in half, right sides together. Stitch ½-inch seam to close one short edge (for bottom) and long edge.

2. Fold remaining open edge down 2 inches and iron. Stitch lace or ribbon trim around this top edge, allowing about ¾ inch to protrude over fold, overlapping ends ½ inch on inside.

3. Turn bag right side out. Hand-sew running stitch around bag 1 inch down from top edge. At center of bag front just below running stitch, use embroidery scissors to cut two parallel vertical slits (wide enough to accommodate drawstring ribbon). Take care to cut through top layer of material only.

4. Turn bag wrong side out. Place ribbon under folded fabric, pressing ribbon edge against running stitches. Insert ribbon ends through slits to right side of bag and pull through evenly. Pin ribbon in place.

5. Turn bag right side out. Sew second row of running stitches just below ribbon, being careful not to sew through ribbon. Remove pins. Fill bag with potpourri, pull ribbon ends to close, and tie.

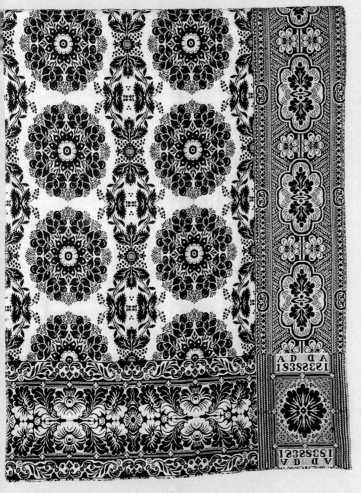

lated the warp threads, Jacquard's device quickly selected and raised the warp threads by a series of punched "command cards" activated by the weaver. More than a thousand cards were needed for a single coverlet.

The complexity and large size of a jacquard loom attachment demanded that the operator be a professional. These weavers were generally tradesmen, who bartered their services, or skilled loom operators, who might establish a business in a town. Women could bring their own yarns—colored with indigo, madder, and other natural dyes—to the weavers and pick up a completed coverlet a few days later.

While standard pattern-book images were frequently used, jacquard weavers also wove personal touches into their coverlets—usually into a corner block. Here a weaver might put his name, that of the buyer, or the date.

Jacquard coverlets were produced mainly in New York, Pennsylvania, and the Midwest from the 1820s until the Civil War era, when increased mechanization forced many hand-weavers out of business.

When evaluating a jacquard coverlet, collectors look for signs of wear, moth damage, and discoloration. A signature and date or a rare pattern enhance its value.

Corner-block inscriptions, such as the "A.D. 1838" woven into the boldly patterned medallion coverlet above left were commonly worked in a reverse-and-repeat pattern so that the words and numbers could be read from either side of the textile. On the coverlet above right, the so-called Boston Town pattern, which depicts colonial buildings and harbor scenes, is combined with palms and pagodas to make a pattern called Christian and Heathen. The border on this coverlet is a double grapevine.

STENCILING ON FABRIC

During the 18th and 19th centuries, itinerant artists carried their stencil patterns and paints across rural America, bringing imaginative folk designs to country homes. Their stenciling techniques remain a simple, inexpensive way to add a personal touch to floors, walls, furniture, or textiles.

The textile stenciling shown here is a fairly straightforward affair: the fabric is laid on top of a placement drawing, which shows the entire design as a guide for stencil alignment. The stencils—one for each different color in the design—are laid in succession on the fabric and used as templates for painting.

Basic equipment for stenciling is available in kits at most craft or art supply stores. Kits usually contain brushes, paints, and acetate stencils (either uncut, as used here, or precut). If you buy the materials individually choose good brushes with natural bristles. For best results on fabric, use textile paint, as it leaves no residue and holds up well to machine washing.

Fine, light-colored muslin was chosen for the stenciling below because it is inexpensive and has good body and stiffness, yet is sheer enough to allow you to see the placement drawing through it as you work. Be sure to use cotton blends or any natural-fiber fabric except wool.

If your stencil pattern is small, use small brushes for better control. After dipping a brush into the paint, be sure to dab off any excess onto a paper towel. The brush should be almost dry before you begin to paint. If your design is multicolored, apply the lightest color paint first.

Follow the steps below to make a small textile piece—a good starting point for a beginning stenciler.

To cut out stencil design, start by placing a stencil on sheet of glass. Holding knife like a pencil, cut carefully along indicated lines, turning stencil as you cut so you are always cutting toward yourself. For neat cutouts, knife blade must be sharp. Repeat process for each stencil.

To make placement guide for proper stencil positioning, tape each stencil in place one at a time on drawing paper and draw along cutouts with marking pen. When design is complete, tape guide to workboard. Stretch fabric taut over drawing and tape in place.

Tape stencil for first color onto fabric, aligning with placement guide beneath. Dip brush into paint and dab off excess paint on paper towel. Pressing stencil against fabric, apply paint with dabbing strokes, working from edges of each cutout section toward center.

MATERIALS

- Textile paints
- Stencils
- Lightweight, light-colored fabric
- Stencil knife with extra blades
- Sheet of glass
  (slightly larger than stencil)
- Fabric-covered wooden workboard
- White absorbent drawing paper
  (slightly larger than stencil)
- Small natural-bristle stencil brushes
  (one for each color of paint used)
- Saucers for holding paints
- Palette knife or spoon for mixing
  paints
- Paper towels for dabbing brushes
- Sponge for cleaning stencils
- Black indelible marking pen
- Masking or drafting tape

Let paint dry, then lift stencil to see if you have applied enough paint. Color should be well defined around edges. If necessary dab on another coat, again using almost dry brush. Be sure paint is dry before removing first stencil and taping on next one.

Repeat technique for all other stencils, being sure to align each new stencil carefully with placement guide. Use new brush for each paint color, and let each color dry thoroughly before removing stencil and proceeding with next color application.

After all colors have been applied and paint is dry, heat-seal paint by ironing each side of fabric three minutes directly with a dry (not steam) iron set for fabric you are using. Trim fabric to desired size for sewing. After use, wipe stencils clean with damp sponge.

Two-headed topsy-turvy dolls are so called because the skirts they wear can be flipped to expose one head and hide the other. First made in the antebellum South, they often feature black and white figures, suggested by the Topsy and Eva characters in Uncle Tom's Cabin. This doll dates from the late 1800s.

Dramatic Designs

Combined with bold originality, the classic patterns in this snug bedroom lend it unexpected drama and character, proving that small rooms do not necessarily call for small-scale decor.

Taking a design and color cue from her striking late-19th-century Pickle Dish quilt, left, the owner devised a series of complementary stencil motifs for the walls. Although stencils are often confined to a horizontal border, these vertical designs work as a unique "wallpaper" to draw the eye upward and visually expand the space.

Above and at bedside, a group of antique needlework and fabric purses adds to the abundance of pattern. To temper the graphic look of all this bright color against white, the homeowner painted the floorboards a smoky gray and added a neutral-tone hooked rug.

The bold wall stencil designs at left were adapted from the motifs of 18th-century New England stencil artist Moses Eaton.

The 18th- and 19th-century purses above add grace notes of color to the large-scale harmony of this patterned guest room. The long folding pouches on the left held needles, pins, and other sewing necessities. The Irish-stitch envelope bags on the right may have been made as love tokens by young women for their betrothed.

Homespun Harmony

Distinguished by a collection of hand-woven textiles, this midwestern bedroom serves as a showcase for the homemade fabrics that were standard furnishings in rural American households until the late 19th century. Known as homespun, these loosely woven materials—generally loomed by women and children from wool, linen, or cotton—were used to make everything from curtains and table linens to coverlets, ticking, sheets, and blankets.

Although homespun fabrics were sometimes woven with elaborate designs, simple plaids and checks were more common because these basic patterns were relatively easy to set up on a loom. Fabrics woven with blue yarns, like those sharing space in the corner cupboard, opposite, and displayed throughout the bedroom, were particularly prevalent during the 18th and 19th centuries due to the wide availability of indigo dye.

The homeowners chose two complementary plaid coverlets for the 1820 rope bed and trundle, above. Pull-out trundle beds—designed with wheels so that they could easily be rolled under the bed when not needed—were often reserved for children. This one is put to frequent use today by the homeowners' grandchildren.

Victorian toys like those above were often modeled on animals and made from whatever materials were on hand. The horse, top, is stuffed with straw, while the buffalo, bottom, wears a wool coat.

Homespun fabrics, once woven as part of the daily household routine, are layered for a rich interplay of plaids and checks in this simple bedroom.

A Dream Porch

The owners of this Minnesota lakefront residence found camping out on their porch so agreeable during the restoration of their turn-of-the-century house that they still sleep there on warm summer nights. Such indoor-outdoor living spaces were commonly used for bedrooms after the late 1800s, when well-ventilated sleeping quarters were first widely promoted.

With nature forming a wraparound wall of color, the decor on this porch takes its cue from the deep blues and greens of the woods, picked up by the painted furniture. Light fabrics continue the open-air feeling: a hand-crocheted spread tops the four-poster bed, which has been angled into the room as casually as a hammock. Lace dresses the adjacent sitting area, above.

Here the informal mood continues: hung on a cord, ticking fabric makes simple country curtains, while the settee and rocker recall the comfortable wicker furnishings that have been used on American porches since the 1850s. Retaining their original finish, this matching set dates from the 1930s. The pie safe, designed with pierced-tin doors to let fresh air circulate around baked goods, now holds china for intimate breakfasts. Built around 1870, the piece originally came from a Moravian community in Illinois.

A leaf-motif stencil trailed above the windows, right, and wicker dressed in floral chintz, above, create a gentle transition between indoors and out on this sleeping porch.

Handmade touches and simple materials enhance the warmth of these cheerful bathrooms. The shower curtain opposite was recycled from an unused quilt front, which the homeowner found at a neighborhood sale. To protect the old fabric, she sewed a muslin backing to it and added cloth tabs for hanging; a standard vinyl liner helps prevent mildew. Wide floor planks, a wood-framed mirror and medicine chest, and an oak toilet seat make rustic counterpoints to the contemporary sink, while a stenciled leaf border adds detail to unadorned walls.

The owner of the bathroom above made plain window curtains out of muslin, creating the delicate "swag" with a string of cranberries. The imaginative candle mount was improvised from an old clothes-drying rack.

In the bright, wallpapered bath above, framed paintings reproduce 17th-century folk-art portraits. The pedestal sink and the porcelain tub are early-20th-century fixtures.

A fanciful departure from more conventional stencil motifs, the painted border above, which reads in full, "Fortune brings in some ships that are not steer'd," was adapted from Shakespeare's Cymbeline.

Pastel colors and a Victorian look characterize these two country-style baths, designed for a pretty, feminine effect. In the guest bathroom above, shell-pink walls and a gathered sink skirt provide softness in what might otherwise have been a severe space. A 19th-century porcelain tea set, simply grouped on an antique scroll-edged corner shelf, adds unexpected charm.

Floral wallpaper, abloom with peonies, and a lace-draped Victorian wicker armchair helped transform an extra bedroom into the luxurious bath at right. The antique lace shower curtain and window curtains lend an air of romance.

Feminine Style

*Colorful botanical prints
framed with bird's-eye
maple accent the floral
design theme established in
the romantic bath at left.
Potted ferns and palms,
typical of Victorian interiors,
thrive in the moist
atmosphere.*

SCENTED FLORAL WATERS

Used in healing and bathing rituals since biblical times, delicate floral waters make elegant scents for both the home and body. Left uncapped, a bottle of the aromatic water will impart a subtle perfume to the air. Lighter than cologne, floral water can also be used as a refreshing body splash. Or added to the tub, it will turn an ordinary bath into a luxurious soak.

Generally made from water or alcohol mixed with fragrant flower petals or herbs, or with essential oils (extracted from the plants themselves), floral waters are easy to make at home. Most of the ingredients that you will need, including oils, are available from craft stores and specialty shops. Isopropyl alcohol, which acts as a fixative, can be found at your local pharmacy. Some recipes call for using vodka instead of isopropyl alcohol; however, floral waters made with vodka quickly lose their scent.

For storage, choose pretty bottles with tight-fitting stoppers or caps, and rinse the containers thoroughly before filling them. Be sure to shake the mixtures well before each use. Any trace of alcohol that is noticeable when a floral water is first opened will quickly dissipate, leaving a refreshing scent.

Floral waters will keep for several months at room temperature, and even longer if you store them in the refrigerator or bottle them in opaque containers.

ROSE WATER

The 16th-century English botanist John Gerard described rose water as "good for the strengthening of the heart and refreshing of the spirits."

- 32 ounces distilled water -
- ¼ ounce rose oil -

Combine distilled water and rose oil in jar. Shake well and let steep for a week. Transfer to decorative bottle.

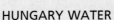

HUNGARY WATER

The original recipe for Hungary Water, said to have been developed for Queen Elizabeth of Hungary in the 14th century, called for distilling the leaves and flowers of rosemary with aqua vitae. This honey-colored floral water has a pleasant citrus scent. It should be made with fresh, not dried, herbs.

- 4 tablespoons fresh mint leaves -
- 4 tablespoons fresh rosemary leaves -
- 8 ounces isopropyl alcohol -
- 16 ounces rose water (see recipe above) -
- 4 teaspoons each grated orange and lemon peel -

Combine all ingredients in jar. Shake well and let steep for a week at room temperature, shaking every day. Strain through fine cheesecloth and pour into decorative bottle.

Antique toiletries make lovely accessories for a bath. The stenciled tortoise shell comb and the hand-painted comb made of horn, top, both date from the mid-19th century. The striped brush, bottom left, was made in New England and was used to smooth delicate trimmings such as feathers. The brush at bottom right kept felt hats groomed.

Drawing their country spirit from imaginative wall treatments, the designs for these handsome baths focus on materials and decorative details. In the rustic bathroom above, located in a reproduction 18th-century farmhouse, pine paneling recalls a type of wainscoting that commonly appeared in the 1700s. Such facing was often combined with an upper wall of whitewashed plaster. The framed fraktur painting is an example of the hand-decorated documents made by the Pennsylvania Dutch.

Two contrasting wallpapers can also create the effect of wainscoting. The owners of the bathroom at right used striped paper and a floral pattern, joining them with a wooden chair rail painted a unifying green. The unusual mirror collection includes one from the 19th century painted with flowers and birds, a tin mirror with attached comb box, a three-part beveled shaving mirror from the early 20th century, and, hung over the sink, a wood-framed plate glass mirror from the turn of the century.

In the pine wainscoted bath above, a late-19th-century doll's dresser, used for storage, is topped by a miniature kerosene lamp and an antique razor box.

In the intimate setting at left, a French wallpaper border picks up the color of the blue-gray floor. Wall lamps of brass and frosted glass are replicas of those from the late 19th century. The marble sink with ball-and-claw feet dates from 1887.

CRAFTING A FABRIC-COVERED SCREEN

Decorative and versatile, a fabric-covered folding screen can conceal clutter, camouflage an unattractive fixture, or create a private dressing area in a bathroom or bedroom. Plaid, striped, or floral print fabrics—chintz or nonstretch cotton is best—will give a country feeling. For two screens in one, pick contrasting patterns for front and back. Just reverse the screen to produce a new look for your room.

A. Stretched evenly over door, back fabric should lie flat, and tacks should be spaced evenly ⅛ inch in from edges.

MATERIALS

· 4 hollow-core doors, 18 inches x 72 inches x 1⅜ inches ·
(a stock size available at lumber yards or home improvement stores)

· 4½ yards fabric, 45 inches wide, for screen front ·

· 4½ yards fabric, 45 inches wide, for screen back ·

· Six 2-inch brass double-action hinges ·
(no wider than 1⅜ inches)

· 250 #6 upholstery tacks ·

· 250 decorative brass studs ·

◆

DIRECTIONS

1. Iron fabric flat.

2. Using fabric for back of screen, cut four rectangles, each measuring 20 inches x 74 inches.

3. Using fabric for front of screen, cut four rectangles, each measuring 22 inches x 76 inches.

4. Spread one piece of fabric for back smoothly on floor, wrong side up. Center a door on fabric.

5. Bring excess fabric around sides of door and secure with one tack at center on all four sides. Moving toward corners and alternating sides for even stretch, hammer tacks at 3-inch intervals, placing them ⅛ inch in from fabric edge (Illustration A). Gently pull the fabric taut as you work. Leave a space open at each corner to make tuck.

6. At corners, fold fabric into neat self-tuck flush with edge (hospital corner). Tack to secure.

7. Using fabric for screen front, spread one piece smoothly on floor, wrong side up. Center door you are working on, uncovered side down, on fabric.

8. Proceeding in same manner as for back, but using studs, fold fabric around sides of door (already covered with fabric for back). Fold raw fabric edges under so that fold line is flush with edges of door sides. Secure fabric with studs placed ⅛ inch from folded edge at 3-inch intervals. Fold and secure corners in same manner as for back (Illustration B).

9. Repeat above steps to make three remaining screen panels.

10. To attach hinges, place them 15 inches from top and bottom of door in space between studs and mark positions for screws. Hammer pilot holes through fabric. Screw hinges into place (Illustration C).

B. With raw edge folded under, front fabric should overlap back fabric flush with edges of door. Tuck in corners.

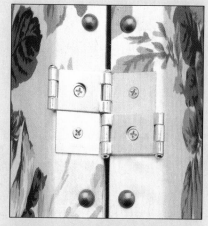

C. Double-action hinges, which enable screen to fold two ways, should be centered between studs.

Painterly Touches

Inventive paint treatments give colorful distinction to these two contemporary country-style bathrooms. A vine of sweet peas, the homeowner's favorite flower, was designed by a professional artist to frame the mirror opposite. Applied with sign-painter's enamel, the flowers not only transform the standard medicine-cabinet mirror, but introduce a cheery decorative element into the simple room. The drawers of the birch vanity were also painted— to mark *hers* with bows and *his* with bow ties. Initials on the doors below further personalize the marble-topped cabinet.

Added country flavor comes from the freshly enameled pine wainscoting that faces the tub,

backs the shower stall, and extends up the wall to encompass a "porthole" window.

In the bathroom above, a stenciled shell-and-bar pattern turns a plain oak floor into a showpiece. The pale background color was achieved by pickling, a process in which the floorboards are first sanded clean, then hand-rubbed with white pigment for a smooth, creamy effect. The owner applied the stenciled pattern with a quick-drying varnish-based japan paint to prevent smearing. She stenciled the bar repeats first, and then added the scallop shells in random tones and in odd directions for variety. Pink and teal were the colors chosen to complement the tub backsplash of French ceramic tiles.

Ceramic soap dishes like the English pieces above were usually part of a toilette set that included chamber pot, basin, slop jar, pitcher, shaving cup, and toothbrush holder. The soap dish at top, made by the Garrett & Copeland Company, dates from 1840. The dish below was made around 1830 in Staffordshire.

Muted colors on walls and floors make a soft background palette for playful painted details in two country baths. The flower vines opposite were painted freehand for a rambling effect, while the shell patterns above show a more geometric design approach.

The
Richness
of Wood

Trimmed with eyelet ruffles, simple cotton curtains soften the wood-detailed bath at right. The oak wainscoting was stained and varnished to enhance its natural grain. Painted a cream color to tie the room together, the original pressed-tin ceiling dates from the 1840s.

The natural warmth of wood lends country character to these two baths. Grained oak sets the tone in the room at left, where the antique, mirrored medicine chest, reproduction 19th-century toilet, and vanity were chosen to coordinate with the wainscoting.

The focus of the bathroom above is a walnut mirror dating from around 1880. Typical of the Eastlake style of furniture design, it displays incised, rather than heavily carved, details and is highlighted with black and gold paint.

Dominating the small bath above, the carved oak mirror is flanked by magazine and advertising art, including hand-colored prints from the turn of the century.

The Hall

*small details make the
difference in this serviceable
and versatile area*

The hall as we know it today has diminished in size to a mere vestige of its namesake—the medieval "hall," which served as a central greeting and gathering space. But while the hall may now be small, it still plays an important role in the country home. Not only does it offer the first impression of a house, but it acts as a transition area between indoors and out and provides smooth passage from one room to the next. And even when it serves as a mudroom, for storing outerwear and equipment, its decorating possibilities should not be overlooked.

The first consideration in decorating such a serviceable space is often practicality. But like any other room in your home, the hall also calls for a personal touch. You can achieve a country look simply by placing a row of old bottles on a sunny windowsill. Or by stenciling the stair risers. Or trimming a door frame with a flowered wallpaper border. As this chapter shows, it is the details that can make a big difference in a small space.

An antique bamboo hall stand is the focal point of a country-style foyer.

The large foyer above is furnished with an old wagon seat. Such double chairs could be removed from wagons and used as additional seating in meetinghouses.

Offering an inviting first impression to a spacious Connecticut home, the striking foyer above draws its interest from the imaginative combination of paint treatments used on the walls. To complement the traditional country decor of their home, the owners had a flower pattern stenciled on the wainscoting next to the archway and adapted an early American motif for the urns that flank the closet door.

For a slightly more sophisticated effect, the white walls above the wainscoting were sponge-painted gray—a technique used by country craftsmen as an inexpensive way to simulate marble. To unify the first and second floors, the sponging was continued in the stairwell and in the upstairs hall, opposite. Instead of running carpeting all the way to the top story, the owners had the attic stair risers stenciled.

Decorated stair risers, opposite, extend the floral theme from the foyer to the top floor.

Painted Patterns

The two lovebirds cut from tin, above—and the angel and rooster in the foyer, far left—are reproductions of antique weather vane designs. With their distinctive silhouettes, pieces like these serve well as artwork in small spaces.

Good looks and practicality characterize these two mudrooms, which serve as convenient spaces for changing in and out of shoes and outerwear, and for storing sports equipment. Set under the large window in the hallway at left, a simple painted bench can be a sunny seat or a handy place where baskets be-come catchalls for the miscellany that inevitably collects in such a heavily trafficked area.

In the hall above, a spatter-painted floor not only brings cheerful color to the small space but also wears well. A footed wagon seat is tucked into a recessed nook, where boots are easily stowed out of the way.

Little more than a corner, the tiny hall above serves as an entry to a guest house. By adding a bench,
the owner transformed the recessed alcove into a convenient seating area.

A DOORKNOB COATRACK

This unusual homemade coatrack puts old porcelain doorknobs to an innovative use. Porcelain doorknobs are widely available at flea markets, salvage yards, and shops that specialize in antique hardware.

The instructions that follow are based on using six doorknobs, but you can adjust the length of the board to accommodate any number.

MATERIALS AND EQUIPMENT

• 6 porcelain doorknobs, without shafts •

• One ¾-inch-thick board, 3½ inches wide by 39½ inches long •
(preferably oak or other hardwood)

• Six #6 flathead wood screws, 1½ inches long •

• Six #10-12 plastic wall anchors, 1 inch long •

• Paint or stain of your choice •

• Electric drill with ⅛-inch bit and ¼-inch countersink bit •

• Router with ¼-inch 45-degree chamfer bit (optional) •

• Two 3-inch C clamps • Utility knife • Standard screwdriver •

• Medium- and fine-grade sandpaper •

1. Insert a plastic anchor into opening in base of each doorknob. Trim any excess with utility knife so anchor is flush with opening.

2. On front of board, measure 3½ inches in from one end and mark spot for drilling first screw hole, centering mark between top and bottom of board. Continue to mark board at 6½-inch intervals for five more holes.

3. Using C clamps, clamp board firmly to work surface. Using drill with ⅛-inch bit, drill screw hole through board at each mark.

4. Turn board over. Using drill with ¼-inch countersink bit, countersink the six screw holes.

5. Using router, bevel edges on front of board, if desired.

6. Sand board with medium sandpaper, then repeat with fine sandpaper until smooth.

7. Paint or stain both sides of board as desired and let dry.

8. From back of board, screw wood screws into holes until screw heads rest below surface of board.

9. Screw doorknobs onto screws protruding from front of board.

10. Mount coatrack as desired to suit wall type.

151

The avid gardener who restored this small carriage house as a vacation retreat needed extra room for potting and storage. Because she wanted to preserve the original layout of the 1920s house, she made use of existing halls and corners instead of adding extra rooms.

In the tiny alcove above, an old apple sink now serves as a worktable and an attractive storage place for the dried plants the homeowner uses in her flower arrangements and potpourris. To create a decorative focus for the small space, she placed antique baskets on the spokes of a wooden drying rack.

Messier tasks, such as potting, take place in the mudroom at right, where the painted cement floor stands up well to dirt and water. As decorative as it is useful, a fold-out laundry rack now dries plants instead of clothes.

Tucked into an unused corner, above, an old apple sink filled with dried flowers transforms an empty hallway in a restored carriage house. Located off a back hall, the mudroom at right doubles as a potting shed.

Carriage House Charm

The late-19th-century pitcher above is an example of painted tinware, which was first popularized in the early 1800s. Originally part of a chamber set that also included a washbowl, vessels such as this serve well as watering cans today.

The Porch

*a transitional space
between house and yard for
casual country living*

Perhaps the ultimate expression of domestic ease, the porch has long been a place for leisurely pursuits. Borrowed from the West Indies, the idea of a cool outdoor living space had already taken hold in the American colonies as early as 1700: houses built south of Virginia after that date commonly had a porch or gallery designed to maximize cross ventilation and provide a pleasant escape from hot interiors. By the late 19th century, the airy open porch of the Victorian era had actually become the center of social life during warm weather, offering a comfortable, "healthy" alternative to the stuffy indoor parlor.

The country porch serves a similar purpose today. Not only does it provide a front-row seat to the ever-changing theater of the street, but it can be a stage itself for relaxed gatherings or a quiet spot for watching the sunset. You will find that any simple furnishings adapt easily to this informal place, which deserves the same attention to comfort as the rest of the house.

A game of checkers sets the scene for a relaxing afternoon on the porch.

Versatile Wicker

Versatile and lightweight, wicker furniture can be easily arranged to suit almost any outdoor setting. On the verandah at left, two traditional porch chairs—a straight-backed armchair and an open-weave Bar Harbor-style piece—were used to create an informal sitting area just right for morning coffee. A delicate cutwork cloth gives the simple stained pine table a summery look in keeping with the airy wicker, while the fringed throw rug helps define the intimate grouping within the larger space of the porch.

On the weathered deck above, a matching set of Lloyd loom wicker chairs becomes the focal point of an appealing outdoor dining area. Machine-made from twisted paper fibers, Lloyd loom wicker was introduced in the United States in 1917 by the Lloyd Manufacturing Company as an alternative to handcrafted rattan. Its tight, durable weave, low cost, and streamlined design made this wicker particularly popular in those days, and original Lloyd loom pieces like these still remain in great demand.

Here the chairs surround a table set with floral-patterned china and napkins, which make an easy transition from dining room to porch.

The cool, informal look of wicker makes it especially appropriate for use on a porch. Painted white, two classic armchairs were used to furnish a corner of the wraparound porch at left. Above, a set of Lloyd loom chairs surround a planked table for comfortable deck dining.

Waterfowl decoys, designed
to lure birds into the hunter's
range, also attract flocks of
collectors in search of
valuable woodcarvings. The
late-19th-century brant—
or wild goose—decoy,
above, is about eighteen
inches long and retains its
original paint. A "stick-up"
decoy, it was meant to stand
in marshland rather than
float on water.

A Natural Setting

The owner of this secluded screened porch uses it as a second living room on hot summer days. She selected durable furnishings like the step-back cupboard and the wicker rocker to complement the rustic setting and because she can leave them in place during the winter. The Grandmother's Flower Garden quilt and bull's-eye rag rug—added as warm, softening touches—are easily moved indoors.

When deciding which of her collectibles to display in this indoor-outdoor room, the owner was again careful to choose objects that could withstand the elements. Here, carved wooden animals and duck decoys, and an array of farm gear suspended from the beams above, provide a year-round, care-free exhibit.

Using beams for display transforms a porch with limited wall space into a gallery for such unusual "sculptures" as the wooden stirrup, 1918 farm bucket from Argentina, and sleigh bell, above.

The screened porch at left offers double pleasure: indoor privacy in a natural outdoor setting.

TRADITIONAL LANTERNS

In the darker days before Thomas Edison's illuminating inventions of the 1870s, lanterns—designed to shelter a light source from the elements—were one of the most commonly used types of lamps. Town watchmen carried them on nightly vigils, farmers tended to pre-dawn chores by their glow, and innkeepers hung them outside to signal travelers. A safer alternative to exposed candle flames, and cleaner than primitive animal-oil lamps, enclosed lighting devices were brought to the New World by the earliest settlers: at least three 17th-century Plymouth Colony families claimed a "lant-horn" among their belongings.

Rudimentary in design, early lanterns were typically made with frames of wood or tinned sheet metal and had windows of translucent animal horn, mica, or oiled paper. As glass became increasingly common during the 18th century, it too was used for windows as well as for rounded globe and chimney enclosures. Many lanterns were also fitted with metal reflectors designed to enhance the light source, which was generally a candle or a wick soaked in whale oil or kerosene.

Today, the wide selection of traditional designs available includes antiques and reproductions. The sampling here comprises both.

Four-sided candle lantern of tinned iron, late 1700s or early 1800s

Six-sided lantern with glass windows, late 1700s or early 1800s

Reproduction of c. 1800 English lantern of tinned iron

Wall-mount oil lantern of tin with sunburst light reflector, early 1800s

Reproduction of 1790-1810 theater footlight of tinned iron

Tin candle lantern with horn windows and conical roof, 18th century

Reproduction of early 1800s light owned by abolitionist John Brown

Wall-mount kerosene lantern of iron and tin with reflector, 1875-1900

Reproduction of 1700-1725 wood lantern with pierced decoration

Porch Living

*A 1930s tent-meeting bench
with canvas seats and
a ladder-back rocker offer
casual seating on the porch
at right, the perfect setting for
an indoor picnic. The
large tobacco basket hung on
one window was made
in Kentucky.*

A multipurpose space enjoyed from spring to fall, this wraparound porch houses not only the casual dining area at left, but also the bedroom and sitting area pictured on pages 118 and 119.

Flanked with rustic benches (the folding four-seater was used at Kentucky tent meetings), the long sawbuck table offers plenty of room for impromptu meals. Set with baskets, bandanna napkins, and 1940s dishes, it is ideal for a buffet in country-picnic style.

The two-drawer pine workbench above, which once held crocks and buckets, was removed by its current owners from the pantry of an 1837 house in Griggsville, Illinois.

Baskets, kitchen utensils, and a salvaged carved panel hang from a dowel on the porch above, creating a freeform "valance" over the windows. The workbench beneath provides display space for more baskets.

163

Casual Refinement

Furniture and fabrics in the colors of the surrounding seascape distinguish this carefully coordinated screened porch. Bare of rugs, the pale wood floor enhances the summery feeling and is easy to maintain.

Often a good place for using cast-off furnishings, a vacation-house porch can also be decorated as attentively as any other room in the house. The owner of this porch near the beach made it an elegant refuge by carefully coordinating colors and fabrics.

The air of casual refinement is set by the sand-colored finish on the floor and ceiling, which were stained to match one another. The rattan settee and tightly woven Lloyd loom chairs were painted complementary shades of green, a traditional color for wicker porch furniture. A classic summer fabric, the bold awning-stripe canvas covering the cushions unifies the color scheme.

AN INTRODUCTION TO WICKER

Generally made by weaving rattan, reed, willow, rush, grass, or paper fibers over a wooden frame, wicker is popular today not only for its appealing appearance but also for its versatility. This cool, lightweight furniture, which can be painted or varnished, is compatible with many types of country decor and is available in a wide range of styles.

People relaxing in wicker chairs today owe their comfort in part to a Boston grocer named Cyrus Wakefield. In 1844, Wakefield began experimenting with making furniture from rattan, and he eventually discovered that rattan's inner pith, known as reed, was particularly pliable and could be woven into ornate designs. By the 1880s, bedrooms, parlors, and porches alike boasted elegant wicker furnishings distinguished by intricate weaving that incorporated spirals, curlicues, arabesques, and other exotic touches.

Soon after the turn of the century, however, changing tastes began to call for sleeker furniture forms. In 1917, wicker maker Marshall Lloyd responded by inventing a mechanized loom capable of working twisted paper fiber into a tight weave. Ironically, the uniform designs created by the Lloyd loom process eventually robbed the furniture of the individual appeal that had first attracted buyers. Wicker fell out of fashion in the 1930s, and it was not until the 1960s that a revival occurred.

While wicker continues to be made today in many of the old styles, antique wicker is preferred by connoisseurs. When appraising an old piece, look for a hardwood rather than a bamboo frame, an original finish, and unbroken weaving: repairs generally reduce the value. Labeled pieces, especially those bearing Wakefield's name, are highly prized.

Whether antique or new, wicker requires proper care. Gentle cleaning with a vacuum brush attachment will remove light dirt. A soapy sponge bath and light rinsing with a garden hose is also safe for most types of wicker, except grass or paper-fiber pieces. These can be wiped with a damp cloth but never hosed.

Painted wicker can also be renewed with a fresh coat of color, but be sure to remove loose paint first with a stiff brush. Chemical stripping is not generally advised as the process can damage the wicker fibers.

Rustic Retreats

The friendly mood of the old-time rural porch, where families gathered at day's end to relax, whittle, or gossip with friends, lingers in these rustic retreats decorated with durable porch furnishings that wear well outdoors.

On the cabin porch at right, bright red enamel updates the 1940s rockers and slat-back swing.

Layered over the table, contrasting quilts serve as a country-style tablecloth, and a stoneware jug adds a complementary pattern of checks.

Unpainted log furniture, like the cedar pieces on the deck above, was standard at turn-of-the-century Adirondack camps and is still popular today. Against the weathered wood, the pottery and crazy quilt provide touches of color.

Traditional porch furniture, such as the "peeled-pole" cedar pieces above and the rockers at right, adds country spirit to a rustic porch and deck.

Spongeware—any pottery decorated with a mottled pattern of colored glaze—was produced widely in America at the turn of this century. The blue-sponged pitcher above, about seven inches tall, is thought to have been made in Ohio.

For the house without a traditional porch, a simple deck can be the link between indoors and out. To take advantage of their lake views, the owners of this Minnesota residence added a ground-level deck to connect the house and an adjacent boathouse with the wooded yard that extends to the water's edge.

Sturdy beams function as an open-air roof, defining the space and offering structural support for hanging ·plants and a rustic Adirondack-style porch swing. Depending on the angle of the sun, the overhead timbers also cast

Acknowledgments

Our thanks to Ronald Bricke, Laura Fisher, Lynn Goodpasture, Greeff Fabrics, Inc., Claudia and Carroll Hopf, Audrey and Mark Jackson, Bettie and Seymour Mintz, Richard Raymond, Nancy Clark Reynolds, Rose Cumming Chintzes, Herbert Schiffer, Dona and Fred Schuller, Nancy Serafini, Dee Shapiro, Pam and Don Siegel, Marilyn Simmons, Joy and Bill Thomas, Holly and David Wesley, Kathy and Ken Wilson, Cinda Wombles-Pettigrew, Phyllis Wrynn, and Mary and John Zick.

Third printing
Published simultaneously in Canada
School and library distribution by Silver Burdett Company,
Morristown, New Jersey

TIME-LIFE is a trademark of Time Incorporated U.S.A.

Production by Giga Communications, Inc.
Printed in U.S.A.

Library of Congress Cataloging-in-Publication Data

The Country home. (American country)
Includes index.
1. Decoration and ornament, Rustic—United States.
2. Interior decoration—United States.
I. Time-Life Books. II. Title. III. Series.
NK2002.C59   1988   747.213   88-4842
ISBN 0-8094-6750-X
ISBN 0-8094-6751-8 (lib. bdg.)

American Country was created by Rebus, Inc., and published by Time-Life Books.

REBUS, INC.

Publisher: RODNEY FRIEDMAN • Editor: MARYA DALRYMPLE
Senior Editor: RACHEL D. CARLEY • Managing Editor: BRENDA SAVARD • Consulting Editor: CHARLES L. MEE, JR.
Writers: LAURA CERWINSKE, ROSEMARY G. RENNICKE • Design Editors: NANCY MERNIT, CATHRYN SCHWING
Test Kitchen Director: GRACE YOUNG • Newsletter Editor: BONNIE SLOTNICK
Editorial Assistants: SANTHA CASSELL, SARAH ZIMMERMAN
Contributing Editors: ANNE MOFFAT, DEE SHAPIRO, CINDA SILER • Indexer: IAN TUCKER

Art Director: JUDITH HENRY • Associate Art Director: SARA REYNOLDS
Designer: SARA BOWMAN • Assistant Designer: TIMOTHY JEFFS
Photographer: STEVEN MAYS • Photo Editors: ALICIA HATHAWAY, SUE ISRAEL
Photo Assistant: SIMEONE RICCI • Freelance Photographers: JON ELLIOTT, PHILLIP ENNIS,
PAUL KOPELOW, ALEX LIPPISH, MICHAEL LUPPINO, DAVID PHELPS,
GEORGE ROSS, DAN SPRINGSTON • Freelance Photo Stylist: VALORIE FISHER

Consultants: BOB CAHN, JACQUELINE DAMIAN, HELAINE W. FENDELMAN,
LINDA C. FRANKLIN, GLORIA GALE, KATHLEEN EAGEN JOHNSON, ELEANOR LEVIE,
JUNE SPRIGG, CLAIRE WHITCOMB

Time-Life Books Inc. is a wholly owned subsidiary of TIME INCORPORATED.

FOUNDER: HENRY R. LUCE 1898-1967

Editor-in-Chief: JASON McMANUS • Chairman and Chief Executive Officer: J. RICHARD MUNRO
President and Chief Operating Officer: N. J. NICHOLAS JR. • Editorial Director: RAY CAVE
Executive Vice President, Books: KELSO F. SUTTON • Vice President, Books: GEORGE ARTANDI

TIME-LIFE BOOKS INC.

Editor: GEORGE CONSTABLE • Executive Editor: ELLEN PHILLIPS
Director of Design: LOUIS KLEIN • Director of Editorial Resources: PHYLLIS K. WISE
Editorial Board: RUSSELL B. ADAMS JR., DALE M. BROWN, ROBERTA CONLAN, THOMAS H. FLAHERTY,
LEE HASSIG, DONIA ANN STEELE, ROSALIND STUBENBERG, HENRY WOODHEAD
Director of Photography and Research: JOHN CONRAD WEISER
Assistant Director of Editorial Resources: ELISE RITTER GIBSON

President: CHRISTOPHER T. LINEN • Chief Operating Officer: JOHN M. FAHEY JR.
Senior Vice Presidents: ROBERT M. DeSENA, JAMES L. MERCER, PAUL R. STEWART
Vice Presidents: STEPHEN L. BAIR, RALPH J. CUOMO, NEAL GOFF, STEPHEN L. GOLDSTEIN,
JUANITA T. JAMES, HALLETT JOHNSON III, CAROL KAPLAN, SUSAN J. MARUYAMA,
ROBERT H. SMITH, JOSEPH J. WARD
Director of Production Services: ROBERT J. PASSANTINO

For information about any Time-Life book please call 1-800-621-7026, or write:
Reader Information, Time-Life Customer Service
P.O. Box C-32068, Richmond, Virginia 23261-2068

Time-Life Books Inc. offers a wide range of fine recordings, including a Rock 'n' Roll Era series.
For subscription information, call 1-800-621-7026, or write TIME-LIFE MUSIC,
P.O. Box C-32068, Richmond, Virginia 23261-2068.